FINANCIAL EDUCATION MADE SIMPLE

Bruno Vilhena

BRUNO VILHENA

INDEX

Title: Financial Education Made Simple

Introduction

The Structure of the Book

Why This Book Is Different

How to Use This Book

Chapter 1: What is Financial Education and Why is it Essential

1.1 What is Financial Education?

1.2 Why is it Essential?

1.3 Practical Exercises

1.4 Conclusion

Chapter 2: Personal Financial Planning

2.1 What is Personal Financial Planning?

2.2 Why is Financial Planning Important?

2.3 Steps to Create Your Personal Financial Plan

2.4 Practical Exercises

2.5 Extra Tip

2.6 Conclusion

Chapter 3: Debt Management

3.1 What is Debt Management?

3.2 Why is Debt Management Essential?

3.3 Steps to Manage Your Debts

3.4 Practical Exercises

3.5 Extra Tip

3.6 Conclusion

Chapter 4: The Importance of Saving and Investing

4.1 What Does Saving and Investing Mean?

4.2 Why are Saving and Investing Important?

4.3 Difference Between Saving and Investing

4.4 Steps to Start Saving and Investing

4.5 Practical Exercises

4.6 Extra Tip

4.7 Conclusion

Chapter 5: Financial Goals and How to Achieve Them

5.1 What are Financial Goals?

5.2 Why is Setting Goals Important?

5.3 Types of Financial Goals

5.4 How to Set Financial Goals?

5.5 Steps to Achieve Your Goals

5.6 Practical Exercises

5.7 Extra Tip

5.8 Conclusion

Chapter 6: Conscious Consumption

6.1 What is Conscious Consumption?

6.2 Why is Conscious Consumption Important?

6.3 How to Practice Conscious Consumption?

6.4 Practical Exercises

6.5 Extra Tip

6.6 Conclusion

Chapter 7: Financial Education for Families

7.1 What is Family Financial Education?

7.2 Why is Family Financial Education Important?

7.3 How to Implement Financial Education in the Family

7.4 Practical Exercises

7.5 Extra Tip

7.6 Conclusion

Chapter 8: Common Mistakes in Financial Management

8.1 The Most Common Mistakes in Financial Management

8.2 Why Recognizing and Correcting Mistakes is Important?

8.3 The Most Frequent Errors

8.4 Practical Exercises

8.5 Extra Tip

8.6 Conclusion

Extras (Book Bonus)

Extra 1: Checklist for Expense Management

Extra 2: How to Use the Financial Management Spreadsheet

Extra 3: Activity Calendar

INTRODUCTION

Welcome to "Simplified Financial Education"! This book was created with a single goal: to make financial education accessible, practical, and applicable to your daily life. We know that managing money can be challenging, but we also believe that with the right tools, it is possible to transform your relationship with finances in a simple and effective way.

A lack of financial knowledge can impact all areas of life, from paying bills at the end of the month to achieving your biggest dreams. This book was designed to help you develop healthy financial habits, organize your accounts, eliminate debt, save money, and invest wisely.

The Structure Of The Book

To ensure that learning is straightforward and applicable, the book is organized in a practical structure with elements that simplify understanding and executing the strategies. Here's how it works:

Simple and Straightforward Theoretical Content:

Each chapter provides clear explanations of key financial education concepts. Written in an accessible way, the content helps you understand the "why" and "how" of each topic.

Practical Examples of the Content:

Immediately following the theoretical section, you will find practical examples that show how to apply the concepts in real life. These examples were designed to make learning tangible and relevant to your everyday routine.

Practical Exercises:

Each chapter includes simple and objective exercises that allow you to put what you have learned into practice. By completing the exercises, you will clearly see how financial changes can be applied to your routine.

Practical Examples of the Exercises:

To ensure you are on the right path, we have added practical examples of answers or solutions. These serve as a reference and make it easier to adapt the ideas to your personal context.

Extras (Exclusive Bonuses):

As a complement to the content, the book provides valuable tools that will transform your financial journey:

Expense Control Checklist: A practical list to review and eliminate unnecessary expenses.

Ready-to-Use Spreadsheet: An easy-to-use spreadsheet, ideal for organizing income, expenses, and investments.

Application Calendar: A simple and practical schedule that organizes tasks and actions over the weeks, helping you progress with discipline and consistency.

Why Is This Book Different?

This is not just another book about financial education. It was designed to be a practical tool, a guide that you can use immediately. With a simple and structured approach, you will learn to handle money consciously and efficiently, without complications.

The greatest differentiator of this book is its **practical application:** at the end of each chapter, you will not only understand the financial concepts but also know how to take action to transform your financial life.

How To Use This Book

Read each chapter carefully and reflect on the presented concepts.

Study the practical examples to understand how to apply the ideas in your daily life.

Complete the practical exercises at the end of each chapter. They are designed for you to put the knowledge into action.

Use the examples of the exercises as a reference and adjust them to suit your reality.

Take advantage of the provided extras (checklist, spreadsheet, and calendar) to create a simple and effective financial organization system.

Ready to transform your finances?

This book is your step-by-step guide to developing the financial education you've always wanted. The change starts now, and with the practical tools you'll find here, you will take control of your finances and bring your goals within reach.

Enjoy the journey, and much success!

CHAPTER 1
WHAT IS FINANCIAL EDUCATION AND WHY IS IT ESSENTIAL

CHAPTER 1: WHAT IS FINANCIAL EDUCATION AND WHY IS IT ESSENTIAL

What is Financial Education?

Financial education is the ability to understand, plan, and manage financial resources consciously and strategically. It's not just about saving money but about making choices that reflect your goals and priorities, both in personal life and business.

It's essential because money permeates almost all important decisions we make—from paying bills to investing in business growth or achieving dreams like owning a house or taking a vacation. Without financial education, these decisions are often impulsive, driven by emotions or misinformation, which can lead to debt, lack of planning, and frustration.

When you learn to organize your finances, you understand the value of your money and begin to use it as a tool to achieve your goals. Financial education isn't just about numbers; it's about building a healthy relationship with money.

Why is it Essential?

- **Prevents Debt Problems:**
  By prioritizing expenses and planning, you avoid overusing credit or unnecessary loans.
- **Helps Build Reserves:**
  Good financial management allows you to create an emergency fund for unforeseen circumstances.
- **Enables Conscious Decision-Making:**
  You start evaluating risks and benefits before making significant financial decisions.
- **Promotes Personal and Business Growth:**
  For entrepreneurs, financial education is crucial to maintaining a sustainable business ready for growth.

Practical Example of the Content

Imagine you receive a salary increase or extra profit from your business. Without financial education, it's likely this money would be spent impulsively on shopping, entertainment, or unplanned upgrades. However, someone with financial education would use these funds to reinforce an emergency reserve, invest in something with a return, or pay off debts. The result? Greater financial security and a higher capacity to achieve long-term goals.

Another example: A small business decides to buy new equipment without analyzing the impact on cash flow. After the purchase, they realize they don't have enough money to cover fixed expenses. With financial education, this decision would be based on clear ROI calculations and planning, avoiding financial crises.

Practical Exercises

Exercise 1: Understand Your Relationship with Money

Answer the following questions:

- What was the last significant financial decision you made?
- Do you think it was well-planned or impulsive? Why?
- What was the impact of this decision on your budget?

Reflection:
Write down what you would do differently today with the knowledge you are gaining.

Practical Example for Exercise 1:
Someone decided to purchase a high-end smartphone on a 12-month credit plan without analyzing its impact on their budget. After completing the exercise, they realized they could have waited a few months, saved part of the cost, and negotiated a discount for a cash purchase. This reflection highlights the importance of planning future purchases.

Exercise 2: Track Your Daily Expenses

For one week, record ALL your expenses, categorizing them as:

- **Essential:** Rent, transportation, basic food.
- **Important:** Courses, work tools, moderate entertainment.
- **Non-Essential:** Impulse purchases, frequent dining out.

At the end of the week:

- Analyze how much you spent in each category.
- Identify areas where you can save.

Practical Example for Exercise 2:
An entrepreneur tracked their expenses for a week and realized they were spending $400 a month on coffee outside the office. By replacing the habit with brewing coffee at work, they saved this amount, which was redirected to start an emergency fund.

Exercise 3: Assess Your Financial Goals

Write down three financial goals you'd like to achieve in the coming months (personal or business-related).
Examples: Build an emergency fund, pay off debts, or save for investments.

For each goal, answer:

- How much money will be needed?
- What is the timeline to achieve it?
- What can you start doing today to achieve it?

Break the goal into smaller steps and create an action plan.

Practical Example for Exercise 3:
Goal: Build an emergency fund of $6,000 in 6 months.
Breakdown: Save $1,000 per month.
Action: Reduce unnecessary costs and allocate 10% of monthly

income directly into savings.

Chapter Conclusion

Financial education isn't something we learn overnight—it's a continuous process of reflection, learning, and adjustment. The first step is understanding how you relate to money and how your decisions impact your quality of life and goals.

From this chapter onward, you will have practical tools to start transforming your financial life. No matter your current situation, there is always room to improve and build a more secure and prosperous future.

Let's take the next step together!

CHAPTER 2: PERSONAL FINANCIAL PLANNING

What is Personal Financial Planning?

Personal financial planning is the process of organizing your finances to ensure you are in control of your money, rather than money controlling you. It involves mapping out income, expenses, and financial goals and creating strategies to balance finances, save, and invest consciously.

This planning is not about "tightening the belt" or sacrificing everything. Instead, it's about prioritizing what truly matters, aligning financial habits with short, medium, and long-term goals.

Why is Financial Planning Important?

- **Money Control:**
  Knowing exactly where your money goes prevents unpleasant surprises.
- **Debt Elimination:**
  A solid plan helps pay off debts more quickly.
- **Financial Security:**
  It builds a foundation to handle unexpected events, such as medical emergencies or unforeseen expenses.
- **Achieving Dreams:**
  With planning, you can achieve important goals such as traveling, buying a home, or investing in education.

Practical Example of the Content

Imagine earning $5,000 per month but always ending the month with zero balance or in the red. By creating a financial plan, you discover that you spend $800 dining out and $500 on impulse purchases. Adjusting these two habits allows you to save $1,300 monthly, which can be directed to paying off debt or building an emergency fund.

Another example: A person who wants to save for an international trip in 12 months. Without planning, they "try to save" but never reach the necessary amount. With financial planning, they break down the total trip cost into monthly savings goals and adjust their expenses to meet the target.

Steps to Create Your Personal Financial Plan

1. **Map Your Income and Expenses:**

    - List all sources of income (salary, extra income, etc.).
    - Categorize expenses: fixed, variable, and extra.
2. **Set Priorities:**
    - Separate essential from non-essential expenses.
3. **Create a Budget:**
    - Use the 50-30-20 rule as a guide:
        - 50% for needs (rent, bills, food).
        - 30% for wants (entertainment, shopping).
        - 20% for savings/investments.
4. **Monitor Regularly:**
    - Review your plan monthly and make adjustments as needed.

Practical Exercises

Exercise 1: Mapping Income and Expenses

Using a notebook, spreadsheet, or app, record:

- All your income (salary, extra income, etc.).
- All your expenses, divided into:
    - **Fixed:** Rent, transportation, basic bills.
    - **Variable:** Food, entertainment, shopping.
    - **Extras/Unexpected:** Emergencies, repairs.
- Calculate the difference:
  Income - Expenses = Final Balance.
  If negative, identify areas to cut back.

Practical Example for Exercise 1:
Monthly Income: $4,500.
Fixed Expenses: $2,000 (rent, bills, transportation).
Variable Expenses: $1,200 (food, entertainment).

Extra Expenses: $800 (repairs).

Final Balance: -$500.

Action: Reduce variable expenses (e.g., fewer dining out) and create an emergency fund.

Exercise 2: Creating a Monthly Budget

Using the values from the previous exercise, apply the 50-30-20 rule:

- 50% for basic needs.
- 30% for entertainment and personal expenses.
- 20% for savings and investments.

  Adjust your expenses to fit these percentages.

Practical Example for Exercise 2:
Income: $5,000.

- **Needs (50%):** $2,500.
- **Wants (30%):** $1,500.
- **Savings (20%):** $1,000.

  Action: If spending on wants exceeds 30%, reduce it to allocate more to savings.

Exercise 3: Planning Financial Goals

Choose a personal financial goal (e.g., travel, debt repayment, emergency fund).

Answer the following:

- How much money do you need to achieve this goal?
- What is the timeline to achieve it (months/years)?
- How much do you need to save each month?

Break the goal into smaller steps and adjust your budget to achieve it.

Practical Example for Exercise 3:

Goal: Build an emergency fund of $9,000 in 12 months.

- **Breakdown:** $9,000 ÷ 12 months = $750/month.
- **Adjustment:** Reduce leisure expenses and direct this saving to the fund.

Extra Tip

Use digital tools to track your finances. Many free apps can help categorize expenses, monitor spending, and even send alerts to keep you on budget.

Chapter Conclusion

Personal financial planning is the first step toward achieving stability and financial security. With organization and discipline, you can transform your relationship with money and direct it toward what truly matters.

No matter your current income or situation—it's always possible to start. The exercises in this chapter are designed to help you take the first steps. Remember: what matters is not the size of the step but the correct direction. Let's move forward together!

CHAPTER 3: DEBT MANAGEMENT

What is Debt Management?

Debt management is the process of identifying, organizing, and strategically eliminating accumulated debt to ensure it does not harm your financial health. Having debt is not necessarily a problem; the issue arises when it spirals out of control, compromising your ability to pay and impacting your financial goals.

Managing debt is essential to restore financial balance, avoid excessive interest rates, and free up resources that can be directed toward savings, investments, or other priorities. The first step is to clearly understand the size of your debt so you can create an effective repayment plan.

Why is Debt Management Essential?

- **Prevents a Debt Snowball:**
  Accumulated debt generates interest that grows exponentially, making it harder to repay over time.
- **Provides Emotional Relief:**
  Being in debt creates stress and anxiety. Managing debt brings relief and security.
- **Frees Up Resources:**
  Paying off debt allows you to redirect funds toward important goals like building an emergency fund or investing.
- **Strengthens Financial Health:**
  Managing debt is a critical step toward achieving financial stability and prosperity.

Steps to Manage Your Debt

1. **List All Your Debts:**
   Include creditors, amounts, interest rates, monthly installments, and repayment terms.
2. **Prioritize Payments:**
   Identify debts with the highest interest rates and focus on paying them off first.
3. **Negotiate When Possible:**
   Contact creditors to request better terms.
4. **Create a Repayment Plan:**
   Set a fixed monthly amount to allocate toward debt repayment.
5. **Avoid New Debt:**
   Adopt conscious spending habits and avoid using credit without a clear plan.

Practical Example of the Content

Imagine someone with the following debts:

- **Credit Card:** $3,000 with 12% monthly interest.
- **Personal Loan:** $5,000 with 3% monthly interest.
- **Car Loan:** $15,000 with 1.5% monthly interest.

This person makes minimum payments on the credit card, ignoring the impact of high interest. By managing their debt, they decide to prioritize paying off the credit card (highest interest rate), renegotiate the personal loan to reduce interest, and keep the car loan payments up to date.

Result: In six months, the credit card debt is eliminated, freeing up resources to pay off the personal loan more quickly.

Practical Exercises

Exercise 1: Identify Your Debts

Make a list of all your debts, including:

- Creditor name.
- Total debt amount.
- Interest rate (%).
- Monthly installment and remaining number of payments.

Organize the list in descending order of interest rate.

Reflection: Which debt is most harming your budget? How can you prioritize it?

Practical Example for Exercise 1:

- **Debt 1:** Credit Card – $3,000 – 12% monthly interest.
- **Debt 2:** Personal Loan – $5,000 – 3% monthly interest.
- **Debt 3:** Car Loan – $15,000 – 1.5% monthly interest.
  Action: Prioritize paying off the credit card, which has the highest interest rate, while making minimum payments on the other debts.

Exercise 2: Create a Repayment Plan

Calculate how much you can allocate monthly to debt repayment. Choose one of the following strategies:

- **Snowball Method:** Prioritize smaller debts to gain motivation.
- **Avalanche Method:** Focus on debts with the highest interest rates first.
  Allocate as much as possible to the prioritized debt and make minimum payments on the others.

Practical Example for Exercise 2:

- **Monthly Income:** $5,000.
- **Fixed Expenses:** $3,500.
- **Available Balance:** $1,500 for debt repayment.
  Avalanche Strategy:
- Allocate $1,200 to the credit card.
- Pay the minimum on the personal loan and car loan ($300).

Exercise 3: Negotiate Your Debts

Contact your creditors and request:

- Reduced interest rates.
- Extended repayment terms (if necessary).
- Discounts for lump-sum payments.

Evaluate the new proposal and adjust your repayment plan.

Practical Example for Exercise 3:

A $5,000 debt with 3% monthly interest was renegotiated to a 1.5% monthly rate, reducing the total amount by $1,200. With the savings, the creditor agreed to a larger upfront payment, decreasing the number of installments.

Extra Tip

Avoid using credit cards or taking on new debts while in the repayment process. Focus on freeing up resources and creating an emergency fund to prevent falling into the same cycle in the future.

Chapter Conclusion

Managing your debts is more than a financial matter; it's an emotional release and a crucial step toward building a more stable life. The process requires discipline and commitment, but the results are worth the effort.

With the tools and exercises presented here, you can begin regaining control of your debts and take the first step toward financial freedom. Keep moving forward—the next chapter will be another key piece in your financial transformation journey!

CHAPTER 4: THE IMPORTANCE OF SAVING AND INVESTING

What Does Saving and Investing Mean?

Saving and investing are the two fundamental pillars for achieving financial stability and growth. While saving involves setting aside part of your income for future goals or emergencies, investing means making your money work for you, generating returns and increasing your wealth over time.

Saving is the foundation for building financial security; it's the "first step." Investing, on the other hand, is the "next step," where you strategically use the money saved to grow your wealth and achieve larger goals, such as buying a house, funding your children's education, or securing a comfortable retirement.

Why Are Saving and Investing Important?

- **Financial Security:**
  An emergency fund protects against unexpected events, such as health issues or loss of income.
- **Wealth Growth:**
  Smart investments grow your money exponentially, outpacing inflation.
- **Achieving Goals:**
  Without savings or investments, dreams like traveling, owning property, or accessing quality education become harder to achieve.
- **Financial Freedom:**
  Investing wisely can reduce dependence on fixed income sources, such as a salary.

Difference Between Saving and Investing

Saving	Investing
Goal: Short-term security.	**Goal:** Medium- and long-term growth.
Example: Setting aside money in a savings account or digital wallet.	**Example:** Treasury bonds, stocks, or real estate funds.
Risk: Low to none.	**Risk:** Variable, depending on the type of investment.
Return: Generally low.	**Return:** Potentially high, depending on time and type of investment.

Practical Example of the Content

Imagine you receive a year-end bonus of $10,000. Without a plan, the money might be quickly spent on shopping or trips. However, if you decide to save $3,000 for emergencies and invest $7,000, your money begins working for you.

- **$3,000 in an Emergency Fund:** Stored in a daily-liquidity savings account or certificate of deposit (CD), accessible for unforeseen events.
- **$7,000 in Investments:** Allocated to Treasury bonds or shares of solid companies, generating returns above inflation.

Result: Your bonus is used strategically, offering protection against emergencies and increasing your wealth.

Steps to Start Saving and Investing

1. **Build an Emergency Fund:**
   - Save an amount equivalent to 3-6 months of fixed expenses.
   - Use secure financial products, such as Treasury bonds or CDs with daily liquidity.
2. **Set Investment Goals:**
   - **Short-term (1-2 years):** E.g., a vacation.
   - **Medium-term (3-5 years):** E.g., buying a car.
   - **Long-term (+5 years):** E.g., retirement.
3. **Choose Types of Investments:**
   - **Fixed Income (Secure):** Treasury bonds, CDs.
   - **Variable Income (Growth):** Stocks, real estate funds.

4. **Invest Regularly:**
   o   Dedicate a fixed percentage of your income, such as 10%, to investments each month.

Practical Exercises

Exercise 1: Establish Your Emergency Fund

1. Calculate your monthly fixed expenses (e.g., rent, bills, groceries).
2. Multiply that amount by 3 or 6, depending on how much protection you want.
3. Determine how much you can save monthly to meet the goal.
4. Choose where to store your emergency fund:
   Suggestion: Treasury bonds or a digital savings account with automatic yield.

Practical Example for Exercise 1:

- **Monthly Expenses:** $3,000.
- **Emergency Fund Goal (6 months):** $18,000.
- **Monthly Savings:** $1,500.
- **Product Chosen:** Treasury bonds.

Exercise 2: Define Your Investment Goals

1. List 3 financial goals you want to achieve.
   Example: Buying a car in 3 years, traveling abroad in 2 years, retiring in 20 years.
2. For each goal:
   o   Calculate the amount needed.
   o   Estimate the time to achieve it.
   o   Choose the appropriate type of investment (short-, medium-, or long-term).

Practical Example for Exercise 2:

- **Goal 1:** Buy a car ($50,000) in 3 years.
  - **Monthly Amount Needed:** $1,300.
  - **Suggested Product:** A CD maturing in 3 years.
- **Goal 2:** International trip ($20,000) in 2 years.
  - **Monthly Amount Needed:** $840.
  - **Suggested Product:** A fixed-income fund with programmed liquidity.

Exercise 3: Start Investing

1. Set aside a portion of your budget for investments (e.g., 10% of your income).
2. Choose a simple investment product, such as:
   - Treasury bonds (for beginners).
   - Real estate funds (for medium-term goals).
   - Stocks of established companies (for long-term goals).
3. Invest monthly and track your results.

Practical Example for Exercise 3:

- **Monthly Income:** $5,000.
- **Amount Allocated (10%):** $500 for investments.
- **Product Chosen:** Treasury Inflation-Protected Securities (TIPS) for retirement (20-year term).

Result: By investing $500 per month for 20 years, at an average annual rate of 6%, the accumulated value could exceed $200,000.

Extra Tip

Never put all your money into a single type of asset. Diversify your portfolio to balance risk and return.

Use online financial simulators to understand the growth potential of your investments.

Chapter Conclusion

Saving is the first step toward financial security, while investing is the strategy to build wealth and achieve long-term goals. Both are crucial to ensuring a stable and prosperous future.

Start with small steps, adjust your finances, and develop the habit of saving and investing regularly. The important thing is to take the first step today and stay disciplined. In the next chapters, we'll continue to deepen your journey toward financial freedom!

CHAPTER 5
FINANCIAL GOALS AND HOW TO ACHIEVE THEM

CHAPTER 5: FINANCIAL GOALS AND HOW TO ACHIEVE THEM

What Are Financial Goals?

Financial goals are clear and measurable objectives that you set to organize, save, and invest your money. They act as a roadmap, guiding your financial decisions and ensuring you stay on track to achieve your dreams and reach economic stability.

Having well-defined financial goals is crucial because they give purpose to your money. Without goals, it's easy to spend impulsively and lose control of your finances. With goals, every financial decision becomes more conscious and strategic.

Why Set Financial Goals?

- **Clarity:**
  Knowing exactly what you want to achieve prevents waste and focuses your efforts.
- **Motivation:**
  Seeing progress toward a goal brings motivation and discipline to keep going.
- **Financial Control:**
  Goals help prioritize spending and direct resources to what truly matters.
- **Future Planning:**
  Financial goals allow you to plan for a secure future, such as a comfortable retirement or children's education.

Types of Financial Goals

Timeframe	Examples
Short-Term (up to 1 year):	Paying off debt, saving for a vacation, buying an appliance.
Medium-Term (1 to 5 years):	Buying a car, building a robust emergency fund.
Long-Term (more than 5 years):	Buying a house, investing for retirement, building wealth.

How to Set Financial Goals

Use the SMART methodology to create clear and achievable financial goals:

- **S (Specific):** Clearly define what you want to achieve.
- **M (Measurable):** Set a specific value or timeframe.

- **A (Achievable):** Ensure the goal is realistic based on your income.
- **R (Relevant):** The goal should align with your priorities.
- **T (Time-Bound):** Establish a deadline to achieve the goal.

Practical Example:

Suppose you want to buy a car worth $50,000 in 3 years. Without a clear goal, this dream might seem distant or unattainable. Using the SMART method, you define:

- **Goal:** Buy a $50,000 car.
- **Timeframe:** 36 months.
- **Plan:** Save $1,400 per month in a programmed-liquidity CD.

This plan transforms a vague desire into a realistic and achievable goal, organizing your finances to ensure success.

Steps to Achieve Your Goals

1. **List Your Goals:**
   Write down all the financial goals you want to achieve.
2. **Prioritize:**
   Rank the goals in order of importance and urgency.
3. **Break Them Down:**
   Divide the total amount of each goal into smaller monthly or weekly targets.
4. **Monitor Regularly:**
   Track progress and adjust the plan as needed.

Practical Exercises

Exercise 1: List and Categorize Your Goals

- Write down:

    - Three short-term goals.
    - Two medium-term goals.
    - One long-term goal.
- Categorize each goal as essential or desirable.
- For each goal, answer:
    - How much money is needed?
    - What is the timeframe to achieve it?

Practical Example:

- **Goal 1 (Short-Term):** Pay off credit card debt ($3,000) in 6 months.
- **Goal 2 (Medium-Term):** Buy a car ($50,000) in 3 years.
- **Goal 3 (Long-Term):** Save $500,000 for retirement in 20 years.

  Action:
- For Goal 1, save $500 per month.
- For Goal 2, invest $1,400 monthly.
- For Goal 3, invest $800 per month in a fixed-income fund.

Exercise 2: Create an Action Plan

1. Select one goal from the previous exercise.
2. Divide the total amount by the timeframe (in months or years).
3. Identify adjustments in your budget to achieve the goal.
4. Choose an appropriate savings or investment method.

Practical Example:

- **Goal:** Take an international trip worth $20,000 in 2 years.
- **Plan:**
    - Divide the total: $20,000 ÷ 24 months = $840/month.

- Adjust expenses: Reduce costs for dining out and entertainment.
- Product: Invest in a fixed-income fund with programmed liquidity.

Exercise 3: Assess Goal Progress

1. Choose a goal you're currently working toward.
2. Answer:
   - How much progress have you made?
   - Are you on track with the established timeframe? Why or why not?
   - What can you adjust to improve?
3. Record the necessary adjustments and reinforce your commitment to the goal.

Practical Example:

- **Goal:** Build a $12,000 emergency fund in 1 year.
- **Progress:** After 6 months, $4,800 has been saved (80% of the planned amount).
- **Adjustment:** Increase the monthly contribution to $1,200 over the next 6 months to make up the difference.

Extra Tip

Review your financial goals every 3 months. Life changes, such as increased income or new priorities, may require adjustments to your plan.

Chapter Conclusion

Setting financial goals is the first step toward building the future you want. They not only guide your financial decisions but also bring focus, motivation, and discipline along the way.

With the practical tools presented in this chapter, you have everything you need to plan, execute, and achieve your objectives. Remember: big accomplishments begin with small, consistent steps. Now it's time to start turning your goals into reality!

CHAPTER 6: CONSCIOUS CONSUMPTION

What is Conscious Consumption?

Conscious consumption is the practice of spending money strategically, evaluating whether each purchase truly adds value to your life, aligns with your financial priorities, and doesn't compromise your budget. It's more than saving money; it's about intentional spending that reduces waste and utilizes resources in ways that support your personal and financial goals.

In today's world, we're constantly encouraged to spend impulsively. Advertisements, social media, and flash sales make us believe we need things that, in reality, aren't essential. Conscious consumption is the key to breaking this cycle and taking control of your financial decisions.

Why is Conscious Consumption Important?

- **Avoids Impulsive Purchases:**
  Helps you prioritize necessities and avoid unnecessary expenses.
- **Contributes to Financial Balance:**
  Reduces frivolous spending, allowing you to save and invest more.
- **Aligns Spending with Priorities:**
  Ensures your money is spent on what truly matters.
- **Promotes Sustainability:**
  Consuming less and more efficiently benefits the environment and your community.

Practical Example

Imagine you're walking through a mall and see an irresistible promotion: "Buy 3, Pay for 2!" You hadn't planned to buy anything but decide to take advantage of the "deal" and end up spending $300. Without conscious consumption, this decision seems advantageous. However, when you get home, you realize you bought products you didn't need and compromised part of your budget.

With conscious consumption, you'd ask yourself before buying:

- "Do I really need this?"
- "Does this fit into my budget?"
- "Will this expense prevent me from achieving an important goal?"

In this case, you'd likely skip the promotion and direct the money toward something more meaningful, like savings or an investment.

How to Practice Conscious Consumption?

1. **Plan Your Purchases:**
   Always have a shopping list and stick to it, whether at the grocery store or in retail shops.
2. **Avoid Impulse Buying:**
   Wait 24 hours before buying something non-essential.
3. **Prioritize Quality:**
   Opt for durable, high-quality products, even if they cost more initially.
4. **Compare Prices:**
   Research and evaluate options before making a purchase.
5. **Assess Cost-Benefit:**
   Ask yourself: "Does this expense align with my priorities?"

Practical Exercises

Exercise 1: Identify Frivolous Spending

1. For one week, track all your expenses and categorize them as:
   - **Essential:** Necessary expenses, such as rent, transportation, and basic groceries.
   - **Important:** Value-adding expenses, such as courses or moderate entertainment.
   - **Frivolous:** Impulsive or unnecessary expenses.
2. Calculate the total spent in each category.

3. Reflect: Where can you reduce or eliminate frivolous expenses?

Practical Example:

Weekly Spending Results:

- **Essential:** $1,500 (rent, bills, groceries).
- **Important:** $500 (gym, leisure).
- **Frivolous:** $300 (takeout, impulsive purchases).
  Action: Reduce takeout spending to $150 per week, saving $600 per month.

Exercise 2: The 30-Day Rule

1. Before buying something non-essential, write down the item and its price in a notebook or app.
2. Wait 30 days before making the purchase.
3. After the waiting period, ask yourself:
   - "Do I still need this?"
   - "Is this item truly important?"
   - "Will this expense harm any financial goals?"

Practical Example:

- **Desired Product:** New smartphone ($3,500).
- **After 30 Days:** Realize the current phone still meets your needs.
- **Decision:** Postpone the purchase and allocate the money to a long-term investment.

Exercise 3: Align Spending with Goals

1. List your financial goals (e.g., vacation, emergency fund, debt repayment).

2. For every expense, ask:
   - "Does this expense bring me closer to or further from my goals?"
3. Redirect frivolous spending toward savings or investments that support your goals.

Practical Example:

- **Goal:** Save $10,000 for a vacation in 12 months.
- **Adjustment:** Cut down on clothing and takeout expenses ($500/month) and allocate this directly to the goal.

Extra Tip

Use the **50-30-20 Rule** to organize your spending:

- **50% for Needs:** Essential expenses.
- **30% for Wants:** Entertainment, hobbies, personal shopping.
- **20% for Savings/Investments:** Focused on goals and financial security.

Chapter Conclusion

Practicing conscious consumption is a powerful habit that goes beyond saving money. It's about living a more balanced life, prioritizing what truly matters, and eliminating expenses that don't add value.

By applying the exercises in this chapter, you'll see how small changes in your consumption behavior can significantly impact your finances and help you achieve your goals. Transformation starts today: consume consciously, save with intention, and invest in what truly makes sense for you.

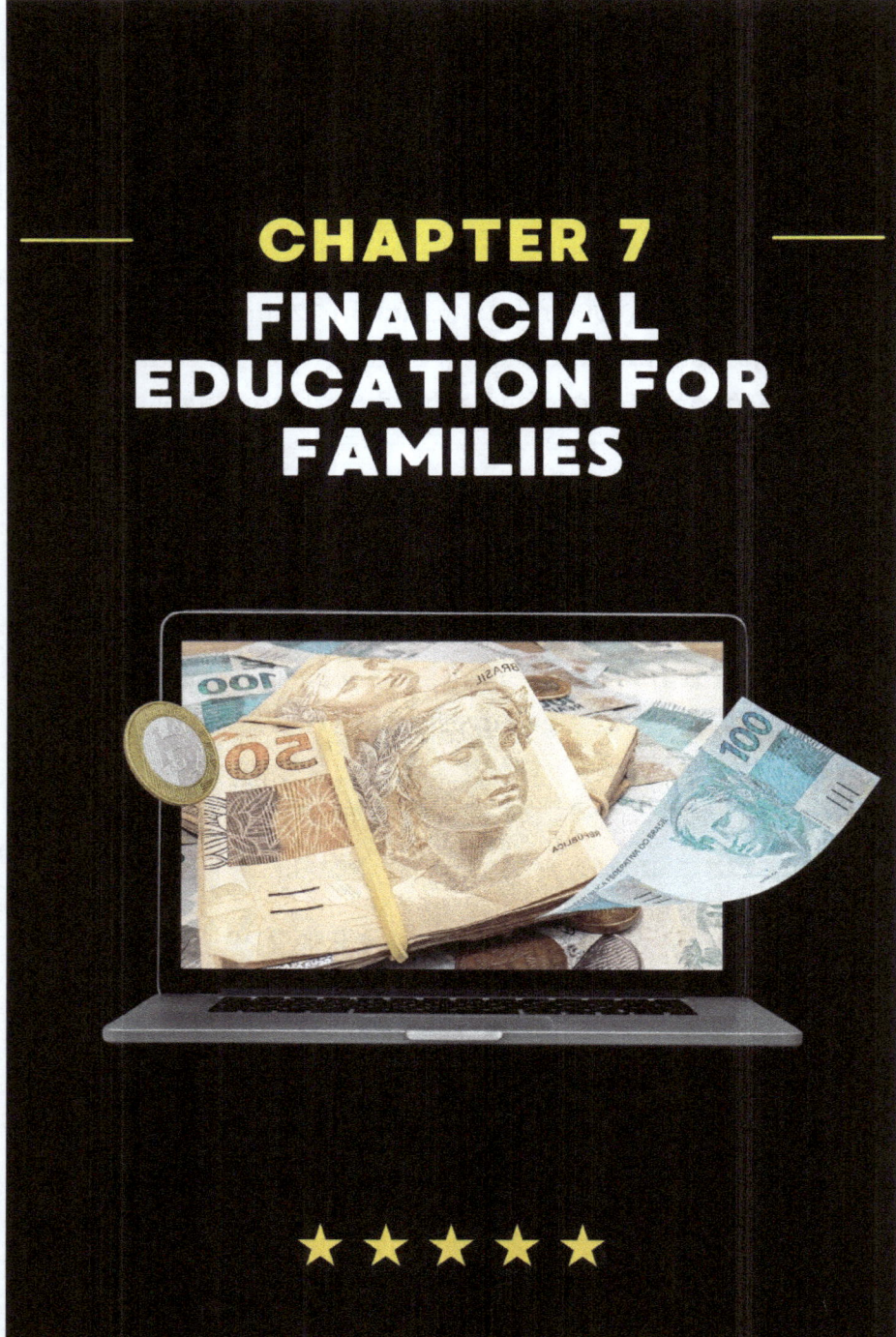

CHAPTER 7: FINANCIAL EDUCATION FOR FAMILIES

What is Family Financial Education?

Family financial education is the process of teaching, learning, and applying financial concepts collectively with family members, fostering an environment of responsibility and cooperation. It goes beyond individual financial planning, involving all household members in building healthy financial habits, planning shared goals, and striving for stability and financial prosperity.

When the entire family participates in financial management, decisions become more conscious, goals clearer, and the emotional impact of finances is reduced. It's teamwork that brings both short-term benefits (balancing the household budget) and long-term advantages (financial education for future generations).

Why is Family Financial Education Important?

- **Promotes Family Unity:**
  Working together toward financial goals strengthens family bonds.
- **Teaches Responsibility:**
  Children learn the value of money and how to use it wisely from an early age.
- **Prevents Conflicts:**
  Transparency and planning make it easier to avoid financial stress and arguments.
- **Builds Security for the Future:**
  Creating a family emergency fund and investing in shared goals ensures stability and peace of mind.

How to Implement Family Financial Education

1. **Talk About Money:**
   Break the taboo and discuss income, expenses, and financial goals openly.
2. **Set Goals Together:**
   Plan shared objectives, such as vacations, home renovations, or paying off debts.
3. **Lead by Example:**
   Demonstrate healthy financial habits in daily life.
4. **Involve Children:**
   Teach basic concepts, like saving and avoiding waste, in a fun and engaging way.
5. **Establish a Financial Routine:**
   Hold regular family meetings to review the budget and

track progress toward goals.

Practical Example

Imagine a family wants to renovate their home within 12 months but has no savings. They decide to:

- Gather all family members to explain the goal and the effort required.
- Analyze the household budget to identify unnecessary expenses (e.g., underused subscription services).
- Allocate a fixed monthly amount to a renovation savings fund.
- Set a "reward" for achieving the goal, such as a special family dinner or outing.

By involving everyone, each family member feels they are contributing to a greater objective, fostering a sense of teamwork and belonging.

Practical Exercises

Exercise 1: Mapping the Family Budget

1. Gather the family and list:
   - All income sources (salaries, extra earnings, etc.).
   - All monthly expenses, divided into:
     - **Fixed:** Rent, utilities, internet.
     - **Variable:** Groceries, entertainment.
     - **Frivolous:** Impulse purchases, unnecessary subscriptions.
2. Analyze the balance:

- **Income - Expenses = Final Balance.**
  3. Reflect: Where can you cut back to save or invest more?

Practical Example:

- Monthly income: $8,000.
- Expenses:
  - **Fixed:** $4,500.
  - **Variable:** $2,000.
  - **Frivolous:** $800.
- Final balance: $700.

  Action: Reduce frivolous expenses by 50%, redirecting $400 toward a shared goal.

Exercise 2: Setting Family Goals

   1. Hold a meeting and define three financial goals for the family (e.g., vacation, emergency fund, education).
   2. For each goal, answer:
   - What is the required amount?
   - How long will it take to achieve?
   - How much needs to be saved monthly?
   3. Divide responsibilities among family members:
   - Example: Parents contribute a fixed amount; children save on allowances or school-related expenses.

Practical Example:

- **Goal:** Family vacation ($15,000) in 12 months.
- **Plan:**
  - Monthly savings: $1,250.
  - Cost-cutting measures: Reduce takeout orders and cancel extra subscriptions.

- Involve children: Encourage them to save part of their allowances.

Exercise 3: Teaching Children to Save

1. Give children allowances (if possible) with clear rules:
  - A portion must be saved.
  - Another portion can be spent on personal items.
2. Encourage them to track their expenses and monitor savings.
3. Create challenges, such as:
  - "Whoever saves the most by the end of the month gets a prize!"

Practical Example:

- Weekly allowance: $20.
- Rule: Save $10.
- Challenge: After six months, the child who saves the most receives a toy or special experience as a reward.

Extra Tip

Use digital tools to help with family financial planning:

- **Finance Apps:** Apps like Mint or YNAB allow shared budgeting.
- **Simple Spreadsheets:** To record goals and track progress.

Chapter Conclusion

Family financial education is an investment in your family's present and future. When everyone works together, the impact goes beyond finances: it creates an environment of cooperation, learning, and shared growth.

The exercises in this chapter are designed to make implementing financial education at home easier. Start small, involve everyone, and celebrate each milestone. Remember: financial success is a team effort!

CHAPTER 8
COMMON FINANCIAL MANAGEMENT MISTAKES

CHAPTER 8: COMMON FINANCIAL MANAGEMENT MISTAKES

The Most Common Financial Management Mistakes

Financial management, whether personal or business-related, is full of pitfalls that can jeopardize financial health and hinder the achievement of important goals. Often, these mistakes go unnoticed until their consequences become critical. Identifying and correcting these errors is essential for building a stable and prosperous financial future.

Common mistakes include a lack of planning, impulsive decisions, overuse of credit, absence of an emergency fund, and negligence in tracking expenses. However, each mistake can be rectified with awareness, the right tools, and changes in habits.

Why Recognizing and Correcting Mistakes is Important

- **Crisis Prevention:**
  Fixing mistakes prevents bigger issues, such as debt accumulation or a lack of resources for emergencies.
- **Continuous Learning:**
  Acknowledging failures allows for course correction and the establishment of healthier financial habits.
- **Financial Progress:**
  Avoiding recurring errors helps allocate resources toward goals and investments.
- **Improved Quality of Life:**
  Efficient financial management reduces stress and increases security.

The Most Frequent Mistakes

1. **Lack of Planning:**
   - Spending without a defined budget.
   - Failing to set clear goals for how money is used.
2. **Excessive Credit Use:**
   - Making installment purchases without analyzing their impact on the budget.
   - Using credit cards as an extension of income.
3. **No Emergency Fund:**
   - Spending all income without saving for unexpected events.

- Relying on loans or credit for emergencies.
4. **Neglecting Expenses:**
- Failing to track where money is going.
- Ignoring small expenses that, when added up, have a significant impact.
5. **Delaying Investments:**
- Believing that a large amount of money is needed to start investing.
- Leaving money idle, losing purchasing power to inflation.

Practical Example

Imagine someone uses their credit card to pay for basic expenses, such as groceries and electricity bills. Without clear control, they accumulate a balance of $5,000 and only pay the monthly minimum, unaware that the 12% monthly interest is exponentially increasing their debt.

By closely monitoring their finances, they could:

- Better plan expenses and prioritize cash payments.
- Build an emergency fund to reduce reliance on credit.
- Negotiate lower interest rates or switch to a different credit card provider.

By correcting these mistakes, they avoid a "snowball effect" of debt and regain financial control.

Practical Exercises

Exercise 1: Identify Your Financial Mistakes

1. List three financial decisions you consider to have been mistakes.
2. For each one, answer:
   o What was the financial impact (positive or negative)?
   o What led you to make that decision?
   o How can you avoid making the same mistake in the future?
3. Reflect: Write down the lessons learned.

Practical Example of Exercise 1:

- **Mistake:** Buying a smartphone in 12 installments without evaluating its budget impact.
- **Impact:** The monthly payment consumed 15% of the income for a year, making it harder to cover other bills.
- **Correction:** Evaluate the total cost and budget impact before making installment purchases.

Exercise 2: Create a Correction Plan

1. Identify a recent financial mistake still affecting your finances.
2. Develop an action plan:
   o List the steps needed to fix the mistake.
   o Set a deadline for resolution.
   o Identify resources or tools you can use.
3. Monitor progress and adjust as needed.

Practical Example of Exercise 2:

- **Mistake:** Having no emergency fund and using a credit card for a car repair ($3,000).
- **Plan:**

- Cut non-essential expenses (entertainment, subscriptions).
- Pay fixed credit card installments.
- Build an emergency fund of $10,000 within 12 months.

Exercise 3: Small Expenses, Big Impact

1. Record all your expenses for one week, no matter how small.
2. Categorize the expenses as:
- **Essential:** Basic needs.
- **Non-essential:** Impulse purchases or avoidable expenses.
3. At the end of the week:
- Calculate the total spent in each category.
- Identify areas where you can save.
- Plan how to redirect the saved money toward savings or investments.

Practical Example of Exercise 3:

- **Recorded Expenses:**
  - **Essential:** $1,200.
  - **Non-essential:** $400 (takeout and coffee shop visits).
- **Action:** Reduce takeout expenses to $100 per week, saving $300 monthly to invest.

Extra Tip

Make reviewing your finances a regular habit, part of your monthly routine. Track your income, expenses, and goals, and ask yourself:

- "Am I on the right track?"
- "What mistakes can I avoid next month?"

Conclusion of the Chapter

Everyone makes financial mistakes at some point in their lives. What's most important is learning from them, creating a plan to correct them, and avoiding them in the future. Financial management is not about being perfect but about being intentional and mindful with money.

With the exercises and examples presented in this chapter, you now have the tools to identify and correct financial mistakes, building a solid foundation for the future. The next step is to continue applying these lessons and commit to your financial goals. Let's move forward together!

EXTRAS 1 - SPENDING CONTROL CHECKLIST

The Spending Control Checklist is a practical tool to help you review expenses, identify excesses, and create an efficient cost-reduction plan. Use this checklist regularly to keep your finances organized and ensure your spending aligns with your financial goals.

☐ Mark for completed
☐ Mark for not completed

1. Monthly Expense Review

- List all fixed expenses (rent, bills, loans).
- List all variable expenses (food, transportation, entertainment).
- Note discretionary spending (impulse purchases, unnecessary subscriptions).
- Calculate the total monthly expenses.

- Compare total expenses with monthly income:
  - **Positive balance:** Excellent! Direct the surplus to savings or investments.
  - **Negative balance:** Identify areas for cuts and adjust your budget.

2. Identifying Discretionary Spending

- Did I make impulse purchases last month?
- Do I have subscriptions or services I rarely use?
- Did I overspend on entertainment or dining out?
- Did I compare prices before making major purchases?

3. Planning Expense Reductions

- Have I separated essential expenses (rent, transportation, food) from discretionary ones?
- Have I set clear goals to reduce spending in specific categories?
  - **Example:** Reduce delivery expenses from $400 to $200 per month.
- Have I renegotiated fixed service contracts (cable TV, internet, gyms)?
- Have I replaced costly habits with more affordable alternatives?
  - **Example:** Cooking meals at home instead of dining out.

4. Expense Monitoring

- Have I used an app or spreadsheet to record daily expenses?

- Did I review my financial progress at the end of the month?
- Did I adjust my budget based on actual spending and financial goals?

5. Credit Card Usage Control

- Did I avoid unnecessary installment purchases?
- Did I pay the full credit card bill to avoid interest?
- Did I monitor weekly card expenses to stay within the budget?
- Did I analyze the impact of installment purchases on future budgets?

6. Savings Strategies

- Have I set a weekly spending limit for variable categories (entertainment, dining out)?
- Did I research promotions and discounts before making major purchases?
- Did I allocate a percentage of my monthly income to savings or investments?
  - **Tip:** Aim to save at least 10% of your monthly income.
- Did I consider free or cheaper alternatives for leisure activities?

7. Monthly Goals and Reflection

- Did I meet my spending reduction goal?
- What was the biggest lesson about my financial habits this month?

- Did I note which categories need more attention for the next month?

Filling Template: Monthly Summary

Category	Planned	Actual Spending	Difference	Action Needed
Rent	$	$	$	None/Negotiate contract
Food	$	$	$	Reduce dining out
Transportation	$	$	$	Evaluate public transport usage
Entertainment	$	$	$	Limit paid events
Subscriptions/Services	$	$	$	Cancel unnecessary services
Other	$	$	$	Review additional expenses

Conclusion

This checklist is your tool for continuous financial control. Review it every month and adjust your habits as needed. Small changes in daily expenses can have a significant long-term impact. Remember: financial control is the foundation for achieving your goals and living with greater peace of mind.

EXTRAS 2 - HOW TO USE THE FINANCIAL MANAGEMENT SPREADSHEET

Congratulations! As a reader of this book, you have exclusive access to the Personal Financial Management Spreadsheet, a practical tool designed to help you organize your finances efficiently. This spreadsheet simplifies financial tracking and empowers you to make more informed decisions.

Follow the steps below to make the most of it, even if you've never used a spreadsheet before:

Step 1: Download the Spreadsheet

Depending on access instructions:

- Scan the QR code provided.
- The file is available in "read-only" mode. To use it fully, go to "File," select "Download," and choose "Microsoft Excel (.xlsx)".

Step 2: Open the Spreadsheet

Open the file in a spreadsheet editing program, such as **Microsoft Excel**, **Google Sheets** (free and online), or other available editors.

- **Tip:** If you don't have Excel, download the file in this format and upload it to your personal cloud (e.g., Google Drive).

Step 3: Filling Out the Spreadsheet

The spreadsheet is divided into sections to make data entry straightforward. Follow these steps to complete it:

Section 1: Income

- **What to Fill In:** List all sources of monthly income, such as:
  - Salary.
  - Extra income (freelance work, rental income).
  - Other earnings.

- **Tip:** Enter net income (after deductions).

Section 2: Fixed Expenses

- **What to Fill In:** Record recurring monthly expenses, such as:
    - Rent, condominium fees.
    - Utility bills (electricity, water, internet).
    - Loan or financing payments.
- **Tip:** Use data from recent bills or bank statements for accuracy.

Section 3: Variable Expenses

- **What to Fill In:** List expenses that vary each month, such as:
    - Food, transportation, leisure.
    - Occasional purchases, delivery services.
- **Tip:** If unsure of exact amounts, estimate based on previous months.

Section 4: Savings and Investments

- **What to Fill In:** Record amounts allocated for:
    - Emergency funds.
    - Investments (government bonds, stocks, real estate funds).
- **Tip:** Ensure these amounts align with your financial goals.

Step 4: Analyze Results

After entering income and expenses:

Monthly Balance

The spreadsheet automatically calculates:

- **Positive Balance:** Excellent! Direct the surplus toward savings or investments.
- **Negative Balance:** Identify areas to cut expenses and adjust your budget.

Automatic Insights

- Expense distribution by category.
- Comparison of income versus expenses.
- **Tip:** Use insights to identify major expense categories and adjust as needed.

Step 5: Monthly Review

At the end of each month:

- Update variable expenses.
- Compare the current balance with previous months.
- **Tip:** Set savings goals and track your progress over time.

Practical Example

Scenario: João wants to organize his personal finances.

- He inputs the following data:
    - Monthly income: R$ 5,000 (salary + freelance work).
    - Fixed expenses: R$ 3,000 (rent, bills).
    - Variable expenses: R$ 1,200 (food, transport, leisure).
    - Savings/Investments: R$ 300.
- The spreadsheet calculates a positive balance of R$ 500.
- **Analysis:** João notices high spending on leisure and decides to save an additional R$ 200 per month.

Step 6: Additional Tips

- **Customize Categories:**
  Adapt the spreadsheet to your needs. For example, create categories like "Education" or "Travel."
- **Use Built-In Formulas:**
  Avoid changing spreadsheet formulas—they're pre-programmed for accuracy.
- **Consistency is Key:**
  Enter data monthly to track progress effectively.
- **Use the "Notes" Tab:**
  Record unexpected events or financial setbacks to understand deviations in your budget.
- **Plan for Unexpected Expenses:**
  Add such expenses to the "Unexpected Costs" section to anticipate their impact on your budget.

Investment Tab

- This tab tracks only the amount allocated to investments—not their returns.
- Use external platforms to monitor investment growth and compare it to your contributions.
- Reinvest the investment returns, and when adding it to the table, treat it as a new investment to build wealth.

Conclusion

With this spreadsheet, you'll gain a clear overview of your finances and can adjust habits to meet your goals. It's the perfect complement to the strategies outlined in this book.

Remember: Discipline and consistency are the keys to effective financial management. Use the spreadsheet as your ally, and watch your financial transformation unfold!

EXTRAS 3 - REALIZATION CALENDAR

This calendar is designed to help you implement the Expense Control Checklist and learn how to use the Financial Management Spreadsheet efficiently, with clear, daily steps.

Week 1: Organizing Finances with the Expense Control Checklist

Day 1: Review Monthly Expenses

- List all your **fixed**, **variable**, and **non-essential** expenses.
- Calculate the total expenses from the last month.

Day 2: Identify Non-Essential Expenses

- Analyze the collected data and identify:

- - Impulse purchases.
  - Subscriptions or services that can be canceled.
- Classify expenses as **essential** or **non-essential**.

Day 3: Plan to Reduce Expenses

- Create an **action plan** to reduce non-essential expenses.
- Set savings goals for the next month.

Day 4: Control Credit Card Usage

- Analyze credit card statements from recent months.
- Identify unnecessary expenses and set a credit limit for the next month.

Day 5: Budget Review and Adjustment

- Using the checklist, revise the overall budget.
- Establish spending limits for each expense category.

Week 2: Learning and Using the Financial Management Spreadsheet

Day 1: Configure the Spreadsheet

- Download and open the spreadsheet in **Excel** or **Google Sheets**.
- Familiarize yourself with the sections: **Income**, **Expenses**, **Savings**, and **Graphs**.

Day 2: Enter Income

- Record all sources of income.
- Confirm net values (after deductions).

Day 3: Enter Fixed Expenses

- Transfer data from the checklist to the **Fixed Expenses** section.
- Double-check the values for accuracy.

Day 4: Enter Variable Expenses

- Input variable expenses (e.g., food, leisure, transportation).
- Use estimates based on past spending patterns.

Day 5: Analyze Balance and Graphs

- Check the monthly balance (**Income - Expenses**).
- Review graphs generated by the spreadsheet:
  - Identify categories for potential adjustments.
  - Plan where to save more effectively.

Day 6: Review and Refine

- Review all data entered in the spreadsheet.
- Adjust your budget based on graph analysis.

Day 7: Reflection and Plan for Next Month

- Write down lessons learned from using the spreadsheet and checklist.
- Set financial goals for the next month.

Summary of the Calendar

Week	Activity	Objective
Week 1	Implement the Expense Control Checklist	Identify and eliminate unnecessary expenses.

| Week 2 | Use the Financial Management Spreadsheet | Organize and monitor income and expenses. |

Final Tip

By the end of these two weeks, you will have complete control over your finances and be ready to make more strategic decisions about saving, investing, and achieving your financial goals. Commit to this calendar, and you'll see transformative results!

ACKNOWLEDGMENTS

ACKNOWLEDGEMENT

I would like to express my deepest gratitude to everyone who contributed to the creation of this book, "Simplified Financial Education".

To my family, thank you for your unconditional support, patience, and encouragement throughout this journey. Your belief in me was the foundation that allowed this project to become a reality.

To my friends and colleagues, who offered advice, insights, and motivation along the way, your contributions were invaluable.

To the readers, thank you for trusting this work as a guide for your financial transformation. My goal has always been to simplify financial education and make it accessible to everyone, and it is you who give true meaning to this project.

Finally, I dedicate this book to everyone striving to achieve financial freedom and live a life of balance and prosperity. Your journey starts here, and I am honored to be a part of it.

With gratitude and respect,
Bruno Vilhena

ABOUT THE AUTHOR

Bruno Vilhena

Bruno M. de Vilhena (@brunovilhena) is a determined entrepreneur dedicated to learning various methods to scale his business.

Diagnosed with Autism, Bruno brings a unique and detailed perspective to the fields of finance and business management. With a story of resilience and accomplishments, he has passed multiple public service exams and served as a police officer in Santa Catarina, where he developed strong skills in discipline and critical analysis.

Currently, Bruno is the Founder and CEO of AEE Clínica Multiprofissional (@aeeclinicamultiprofissional), a clinic specializing in the care of autistic children. His personal and professional experiences have turned the clinic, within just one year of operation, into a market leader in its niche. Bruno inspires other entrepreneurs to adopt solid strategies for business development, offering practical tools to transform their companies' finances and achieve sustainable growth.

www.ingramcontent.com/pod-product-compliance
Lightning Source LLC
Chambersburg PA
CBHW070352230526
45471CB00006B/2533